Knock-Your-Socks-Off Art and Literature

www.kysoflash.com

KYSO Flash online journal

KYSO Flash Press

NEW SHOES

new and selected
haibun stories by

Dan Gilmore

with cover art by

Gwen Murphy

New Shoes: New and Selected Haibun Stories
By Dan Gilmore
Edited by Clare MacQueen

ISBN: 978-0-9862703-5-2
First printing: May 2016
Published by KYSO Flash™ Press, Seattle, Washington, USA

This book was designed and formatted by Clare MacQueen in MS Word for Mac (with covers created in Mac Pages). Interior text is set in Cambria 11 point, with headers set in Cochin 12 and 14 point. Cover text is set in Cambria, Cochin, and Times New Roman. Book design is copyrighted 2016. All rights reserved.

The cover image shows a pair of sculptures by Gwen Murphy, "Manifest Destiny" (Foot Fetish #67; October 2010; http://www.gwenmurphy.com), and appears here with her kind permission. Copyright by Gwen Murphy. All rights reserved.

Please send questions and comments to:

KYSOWebmaster@gmail.com

In memory of Steve Kowit
1938–2015

Poet, social justice activist,
teacher, lover of life, and
protector of the least of us.
His heart was so big,
his light so bright,
that he inspired love,
laughter, and tolerance
in all of us.

Other Books by Dan Gilmore

Just Before Sleep: Haibun Stories
(KYSO Flash Press, 2015)

Panning for Gold: New and Selected Poems
(Imago Press, 2014)

Love Takes a Bow: New and Selected Poems
(Imago Press, 2010)

A Howl for Mayflower
(Imago Press, 2006)

Season Tickets: Poems and Stories
(Pima Press, 2003)

Table of Contents

---

[*] Indicates tanka prose rather than haibun story, and contains one or more tanka (five-line poems) rather than haiku (three-line poems)

✧

Introduction from the Editor

If you adore a good story—one that's well written and well told, one that entertains and inspires, the kind that dazzles and makes you weep and laugh out loud at the same time—then you're in for a treat with *New Shoes*. This wondrous collection by poet and master story-teller Dan Gilmore offers 53 noteworthy stories to savor: specifically, haibun stories, a hybrid form of flash writing[1] which blends prose poems with haiku or senryu.[2]

"Like a Zen slap on the reader's back," Gilmore says, the haiku "enriches, deepens, and expands" the prose.[3]

The emotionally resonant narratives in this book may be tiny (with the shortest running 68 words and the longest, 439), but they address large and universal themes—life and death, love and loss—with penetrating wisdom and insight. Their subject matter and tone range from dead serious, to nostalgic and mournful, to whimsical and absurd, to downright hilarious.

New Shoes is Gilmore's fifth collection of poems and stories. He's also author of a novel, and, not surprisingly, nearly 80 years on the planet have blessed him with an abundance of rich material to draw from. Beyond a myriad of roles as son, brother, spouse, life partner, friend, father, and grandfather, his life experiences also include blue-, white-, and gold-collar jobs from (among others) fry cook to college dean to psychologist—plus, ongoing work as a no-collar jazz musician and creative writer. He calls writing "the hardest and most enjoyable thing I have ever done."[4]

As a fellow seeker (i.e., one who never stops wondering), I enjoy Gilmore's gently irreverent way of looking at life. I also relish the undercurrent of quirkiness and the interplay of comedy and tragedy in his work, his haibun especially, many of which are fables and allegories. They explore the human struggle to make sense of things that often seem incomprehensible, in particular existential and spiritual matters.

In a few, Gilmore plays it serious and somber, while in others, he plays with the absurd, experimenting both with "the garnish of excess" in the telling of the story and with the haibun form itself. In "The Hyperbolist," for example, he incorporates not only senryu but also free verse and tanka[5]—a fine illustration of his premise:

> ...I throw off the reins of propriety. I dance the dance of embellishment. I am addicted to blatant ornamentation and corpulent elaboration. For it's the garnish of excess that tastes so much sweeter....

At *KYSO Flash*, we're keen on publishing boundary-stretching hybrids like these. Innovative haibun may contain imagined realities, narrative threads, or other elements of fiction such as characterization and dialogue to tell their truths, which is why we prefer the term "haibun stories" for such works. In addition to multiple haiku or senryu of various line lengths (one to four), they may also include tanka. Once in a blue moon, we may even see that rarest of hybrids: prose + haiku + tanka. "Raymond's Epiphany" (page 66) is an example of this rarity, and a remarkable story in more ways than one.

The majority of works here in *New Shoes* can be called innovative, stretching as they do the boundaries of traditional English-language haibun, a form which continues to evolve more than 50 years after Beat Poets such as Jack Kerouac, Allen Ginsberg, and Gary Snyder began writing haiku.

While Gilmore has been writing poetry and fiction for 20 years now, his first experiments with haibun began a year ago. In

February 2015, he enthusiastically accepted the *KYSO Flash* challenge for writers of prose poems and micro-fictions to try their hand at haibun stories. One thing quickly led to another, and we were delighted to release his first collection of narrative haibun barely three months later, in May. The 23 works from his chapbook *Just Before Sleep* were then featured in Issue 3 (Spring 2015) of *KYSO Flash* online, inspiring novelist Michael Pritchett to include this commentary in his review of that issue:

> Gilmore's work shows us what the flash form does best and that is dramatize life's flashes, moments when we glimpsed something startling in a park or in a neighbor's window or a friend's face, there for an instant, never repeated or explained...[6]

Last summer, Gilmore was having so much fun that he decided to write four or five dozen haibun stories over the course of fall and winter, or enough for a full-length collection. He invited me to select, copyedit, and sequence those works. Of course, I was thrilled to accept!

As the manuscript neared completion, I began searching online for inspiration for the cover design and soon discovered the work of artist and designer Gwen Murphy, who brings to life in her marvelous three-dimensional works the startling faces and personalities that she sees in shoes. Seems only natural then to feature on the front cover of *New Shoes* two of her wildly original sculptures, "Manifest Destiny." From the beginning, it looked to me as if these expressive characters were wearing hats similar to the mitres worn by certain clergy members. I saw right away a metaphorical connection between this eye-catching visual art and Gilmore's allegories in haibun.

"Manifest Destiny" gives new life to a pair of loafers which belonged to Murphy's husband when he was a stockbroker. She chose the title because it "acknowledges the sad irony of a Native American moccasin style being appropriated for a shoe worn by a white-collar professional."[7]

On behalf of KYSO Flash Press, thanks so much to Dan Gilmore and Gwen Murphy for allowing us to publish their works. Such an honor and a pleasure to present this exceptional book to a world of folks who enjoy a good story.

—Clare MacQueen
May, 2016

Footnotes:

1. Flash works in *KYSO Flash* are up to a thousand words long.
2. Haiku in English are typically three-line poems with a short-long-short line structure, 10 to 17 syllables, a season word, and a juxtaposition between two images from the natural world. Senryu are three-line cousins to haiku that usually highlight the foibles of human nature, often with humor.
3. Dan Gilmore in email to Clare MacQueen; quoted here with author's permission.
4. From Gilmore's biography at: www.dangilmorewrites.com
5. English-language tanka (translated from Japanese as "short song") are usually five-line poems of about 31 syllables and a line structure of this pattern: short, long, short, long, long.
6. Michael Pritchett: "New Online Mag Showcases Wealth of Flash Fiction Forms" in *The Review Review*, June 2015.
7. Gwen Murphy in email to Clare MacQueen; quoted here with artist's permission.

✧

Haibun Stories

If we're allowed even one ping, it should never be a perfect ping,
the ping everyone is expecting and will forget
as soon as it occurs. The unexpected ping
delivered a bit off-beat but with passionate intention
adds beauty and a little sizzle to our sometimes dreary lives.

—Dan Gilmore

*adapted from "The Triangle Player" (a monologue for
Mayflower Bryant) which appears in Gilmore's collection,*
Panning for Gold *(Imago Press, 2014)*

See also: http://www.kysoflash.com/GilmoreTriangle.aspx

New Shoes

He walks out of the Pic and Save carrying his old shoes and wearing his new ones. At first, he's high-stepping like a drum major. But a block away his new shoes feel intensely uncomfortable. They are longer and narrower than his old ones. They don't bend. The soles hit flat on the sidewalk. He veers left, over-corrects and stumbles right. This is dangerous. He hears a chugging sound and discovers each shoe has a little motor in it, and each motor has a mind of its own. He lunges forward to a bench next to a small lake. He takes off his new shoes, puts on his old ones, and tosses the new ones into the lake. He watches them putt away, totally uncoordinated, bobbing this way and that, wobbling their way to someplace he personally would never consider going.

after molting
a bird builds its new nest
with its old feathers

Looking for Something

I shuffled from the bathroom to the kitchen. You stood at the counter pouring coffee. "What are you looking for?" you said. I tried to think of something that might make sense. But nothing came to mind, so I said, "Do I look like I'm looking for something?" And you said, "You're always looking for something."

You handed me a cup of coffee and rubbed between my shoulders. I wanted to say it bothers me that life is so short and filled with so many meaningless moments. But you were buttering your toast. Without looking up you said, "See, you're doing it again."

I excused myself and went back to the bathroom, where I stared into that big mirror that I usually avoid. I saw a bald old man with a furrowed brow and scraggly beard. You were right. The guy in the mirror was definitely looking for something. I leaned in for a closer look. Closer. Our eyes teared up. We touched hands. We smiled. The welcoming smile of two old friends who haven't seen each other in years.

on his way home
he built small fires
with tinder weeds and twigs

Wheels: A Love Poem

Wheels never got me close to love. The fabulous *whirr* made by the playing cards I pinned to my bike spokes before racing by Joyce Clement did not turn her head. The little red motor scooter I thought might place Laverne Carmen behind me, holding tight, hair flaring in the wind, didn't do it. When I *putted* by, all she did was laugh. Six years later I took Barbara Harvey to Mimi's Drive-In in my old '36 Chevy. All she did was talk about the keen '42 Ford next to us, lowered with *purring* pipes and a driver who looked like James Dean. After that came a '55 Dodge and a bust with Linda Fishman, then a '65 Pontiac that missed the mark with Judy Clark. And there was my new Honda Accord that failed to impress the recently baptized Lorna Bernard.

My current mode of transportation is the city bus. I did find love, but not from anything I could start and stop. I stood still long enough and there you were, impressed with just me, no wheels required.

old couple inches along
arm in arm finally
knowing who they are

Overheard in Silverman's Deli,
St. Paul, Minnesota

He: I feel like I've been awake two days.

She: You should take a nap this afternoon.

He: I can't sleep when I don't read the paper before.

She: It didn't come this morning.

He: That's what I'm talking about. Nothing works anymore. Things don't come like they used to.

She: Reading about the world falling apart is no way to get to sleep.

He: It's the best way…. Look at that. It's snowing again.

She: Maybe we should move to Miami like your brother.

He: Hope Vic and what's-her-name don't get frostbite down there.

She: Her name is Kimberly.

He: Yeah, Miss Georgia Peach 1954. How does he do it?

She: She's Alabama Fig.

He: Huh?

She: That Kimberly one is Alabama Fig.

He: Vic told me Peach.

She: That was Brandi.

He: They don't look like they used to. Vic's what? Seventy-five?

She: He's sixty-six, Eddie. He's your younger brother. Remember?

He: Moving there got him going. Down there. Know what I mean? Going south for the wiener, he said.

She: Vic never heard of moderation.

He: You're right. Too much happiness can change a person. Maybe we *should* move there.

She: You got figs and peaches on your brain, Eddie. You ain't suited for happiness. It makes you nervous.

He: I like your hair that way. It's different.

She: I've worn it this way for forty years.

He: I mean it's a little…you know, wind-blown or something.
She: Stop it, Eddie.
He: Pass the salt.
She: You use too much salt.
He: The pepper too.
She: Why don't you ask for the pepper when you ask for the salt?
He: It's understood. When you ask for salt, you are also asking for the pepper.
She: Not by me, it isn't. With me you ask for what you want.
He: That a fact? Okay, let's go home and mess up the sheets.
She: You'd be thinking about Ms. Fig.
He: I'd be rubbing my nose in that new hair of yours.
She: Here's the pepper, Eddie. Finish your eggs. We'll go home. We'll buy a paper on the way. You can read about misery and take a nap. Then we'll see. We ain't moving to Miami though.

heavy snow falls
old ones sit close to the stove
remembering

Visitation

for Steve Kowit

On my walk I took a shortcut through a boarded-up part of town & saw a man sitting at a bus stop. Ballistic hair, swollen feet that tested the strength of his down-in-the-heel Birkenstocks. "This isn't a bus stop anymore," I said. "The bus has stopped coming this way."

He pointed across the street. "Mary & I used to live up there, just above the Wind Chimes Bar: jazz, blues, poetry. Ginsberg dropped by once." Then, as if giving me advice, he said, "Important stuff, this remembering. Cherish it."

I asked where he lived now. He pointed up. "Paradise," he said. "Better than L.A. Not as good as Ocean Beach. I miss that lady there who sells apples. Apples don't taste the same in heaven." He stood, straightened his back, & navigated his way through broken glass, over chunks of cement & bricks, past boarded-up doors. He paused to give a stray dog a pat before disappearing around the corner. The dog followed him. In the stillness I heard the far away cry of a saxophone, the fiery staccato of a poet, & then…the tinkle of wind chimes.

has anyone seen
the man who pounds out lightning?
I need to be struck

Early Religious Experiences

Highland, California: the fragrance of summer's first cantaloupes at Harmon's Grocery. Sermons zealously delivered by Miss Delaware's dog. Pilgrimages to the Texaco to inhale the scents of oil and gasoline. Watching someone use the new pay phone. Drinking a Vanilla Phosphate in Steward's Pharmacy. The library, the Noah's Ark of books. The cherry scent of Doc Greenberg's pipe. The willow in front of his office that actually wept.

They're gone now, buried under freeways, food franchises, and a mall. But like any true believer I still see gossamer proof of their existence every time I fill my tank at the Shell station, or drop a book off at our new library. Today I bought a tasteless cantaloupe at Safeway. I sat on my porch and ate it while, in the distance, a dog whined and a snail inched its way across my driveway to a cool damp spot under a philodendron.

deep under the skin
bruises and shadows conserve
hope for morning sun

Beliefs

My mother believed that if you drank milk with cherry pie, you'd die. Milk with fish was less dangerous, but still life-threatening. She believed that masturbation would make a man blind, insane, and crippled. She believed that women didn't do such things. Once, she believed that on the following Tuesday at 3:37 p.m., Jesus would come again and all good people would be swept up to the heavens. She believed my father would be left behind. That Tuesday morning she prayed and sang and cooked my father a nice goodbye breakfast. She even gave him a goodbye peck on the cheek. When Jesus didn't come, she blamed my dad.

I'm an old man now, and I've discovered I'm capable of coming up with a belief about practically anything, especially things I know nothing about. I can even believe in an afterlife and not believe in it at the same time. And, I'm happy to report that my eyesight is reasonably good and I still have my wits about me. However, I do have a slight limp, I'm still a little queasy about drinking milk with cherry pie, and every Tuesday I glance up at 3:37 to see if anything is stirring.

> snowplow rumbles
> down the street, then drifts
> away into silence

The God of the Pepper Tree

We didn't have pepper trees in Oklahoma, where I was born, but in California one grew outside my window, tall and filled with yearning. Its leaves flickered in sunlight like small wings. At night the tree dropped its red pepper-seeds on the roof to remind me that I was king of this carnival world of sunshine and oranges. And every afternoon I would climb high, straddle a limb, and imagine myself invisible and all-powerful. I looked down on a world where Mr. Peterson and his dog were shepherd and flock. Where Miss Nichols beat dust from her rug and became my appointee to my court of clouds. And all the world danced beneath me, existed only to please me. After a while, my mother would come, stand beneath me, and offer up her prayer: *Danny, come down from there and eat your dinner.* And I would descend, back into the world of bone and flesh and clacking tongues where my father would pass the beans and cornbread with no idea he was offering them to the god of the pepper tree.

children playing
breathless laughter takes flight
on the wings of life

Big Boy

In the fifth grade, a new boy came to church. They called him, *that Big Boy*. He sat in the back row with his mother. He chewed his tongue and wore a banged-up blue helmet. His arms serpentined wildly. He had a hard time walking. At unexpected times he'd lean back and howl like a dog. When my mother told me he got that way because he played with himself, I began to feel the urge to howl. Then one Sunday Big Boy's mother helped him up the aisle to be baptized. He jerked and flung himself forward like a fish being reeled in. As he and the minister entered the baptismal, I prayed that being baptized would help Big Boy. If it cured him, I had a chance to escape my own fate. But when the minister lowered him into the water, Big Boy made gurgling sounds and flailed about trying to grab hold of his penis. But he couldn't. Next day Big Boy and his mother moved away. And for years I waited in terror for my own helmet, my crippled legs, my howl.

on a spring morning
a leaf falls in the back yard
no fear, no sense of fate

On Easter Morning

A little girl named Quin watches her cat play with a cricket. The cat pretends to ignore it, and then, as if seeing it for the first time, pounces and bats the creature with a flick of its paw. The little girl knows she can put the cricket out of its misery, but it is still trying to make a chirping sound with the one leg remaining. Finally, the cat goes away, and on her hands and knees, Quin watches the cricket's one leg quiver. She smashes it with her hand and carries the carcass to the back yard. Standing there with the dead cricket in the palm of her hand, she sees a purple nub of iris which has broken through the cold crust of winter.

> bare plum tree
> the child asks
> where are the plums

Lazarus Ponders His Resurrection

I heard a voice. *Lazarus, come forth!* My feet were cold, but I managed to wiggle my toes. Flickers of warmth moved up my legs, my torso, my neck and face. I peered through dusty light at silhouettes of people standing nearby. A woman helped me remove the sheet that bound me. *What's going on?* I whispered. "You died," she said. She pointed to a young man. "And that one resurrected you with his words. He made a miracle." I said nothing but wondered why a young man with such powerful words couldn't also give me a set of good teeth, take care of my limp, and heal the boil festering on my neck. As far as I could tell, I was the same miserable me I was before resurrection. "You must spread the word," the woman said. "What word?" I said.

Even though I spent a week thinking about resurrection, my thoughts were the same as before I died. *The olives are small this year. Should I even bother picking them? This aching tooth is killing me! Why wasn't I invited to the wedding festival like everyone else?* And gawkers, so many gawkers coming to stare at me. The only thing I could figure was, maybe living is about learning to suffer and, of course, to suffer you need a body. So that's the message I gave gawkers. It didn't go over all that well.

The young man left. I heard they put him on the cross and three days later he self-resurrected and went to a nice place called heaven. This made me wonder why I didn't go to this nice place also. On the cross the young man said something about forgiving us because we don't know what we're doing. He got that right. We don't have a clue. If he ever shows up here again, I'll ask him about this resurrection business. Between you and me, I don't see much good in it.

Mother says, I gave you life
Father says, I gave you life
Baby looks puzzled

Happiness

Eddie's mother ran off with a Nazarene, the Reverend Norman Ranger. Rode away happy as a pup on the back of his Harley. Her red hair sparkled in the sunlight. The last thing she said to Eddie was, "Promise me you won't grow up to be like your father."

He watched until they disappeared over the hill and the dust settled. He didn't know how he felt about preachers on motorcycles. Seemed like gravy on ice cream. His father called the Nazarene a heathen liar. He didn't shed a tear when, a week later, they ran off the hundred-foot-high Cedar Creek bridge. "Died instantly," the doctor said, as if he knew something nobody else could know. "Hope not too instantly," Eddie's father said.

Eddie couldn't take it in. He tried to pray for his mother's soul, but his throat locked up. What was she thinking when they ran off the bridge? Was she screaming? Was she terrified? No, impossible. She was smiling, her head pressed to the preacher's back, saying a prayer of thanks for the one week of happiness the Lord had given her.

> railroad tracks
> forever parallel
> never touching

After 9-11

I took a plane from Tucson to Los Angeles. A man of Arab descent sat next to me. When the plane was in the air, he started rocking and praying. I squeezed past him and walked back toward the bathroom. A woman next to the emergency exit was reading the Bible. Behind her a man in a white turban had his eyes closed. In the rear a Buddhist monk clad in orange seemed suspiciously serene. I returned to my seat. The air was smooth. The Arab had stopped rocking. Then we hit an air pocket. He started rocking again. I said my own silent prayer to counter his in case he was praying for us to crash. It worked. The air was smooth again. Later the man turned to me and said something that sounded like, *killing crowds.* Startled, I said, "What the hell...?" He said, "Sorry. I was speaking about the billowing clouds." My heart raced. I couldn't think of anything to say. The Arab began humming. I took a quick glance at the clouds.

two soldiers scream "peace"—
in war the clearest voices
are muffled by fear

Rabbi Kaufman's Thoughts About Suffering

In every consciousness there's a small room for gloom. Some of us have already mastered the art of unrelenting sorrow. Others—broken-hearted adolescents, the couple just back from their honeymoon—are only beginning their studies in wanting what they cannot have. Most of us try to conceal our pain. You have coffee with a septic whiner and discover his whining awakens in you your own misery. And even though you are more interested in your own wretchedness, you ask, "Are you all right?" to which he answers, "Oh, yes. I'm fine, just fine. How about you?" And you, of course, answer in kind, "Fine, very good." The dark waters of suffering run deep. They wash over palaces and yachts, gravel pits and fire-snorting blowhards, bedrooms and pulpits. No matter what the Buddhists say, suffering is inescapable. So, here's my advice. The true master likens suffering to a Laurel and Hardy pratfall. He sees it coming, he knows it's going to hurt, but when it happens, maybe in a small way, it's funny. God is indeed a practical joker. The trick is to snicker a little and try not to cry out loud. Then there's always Prozac.

along every road
dented mailboxes
reach out

{The author thanks Louis Jenkins for the mailbox image.}

✧

Dark Angel

Sister Madeline's mind won't stay on track. She no longer feels God's presence. A dark angel hovers over her wherever she goes. Once, she dreamed of being a writer, an interpreter of holy scripture, but she turned out to be a reader, a school teacher, and not a very good one at that. Now, at 2:30 a.m., she sits in her room reading a poem by Anne Sexton called "Cockroach." She shivers at the thought of those filthy things. A line strikes her. Vapors of fear engulf her as she reads:

> Yet I know you are only the common angel
> turned into, by way of enchantment, the ugliest.

The dark angel's wings rustle above her. A cockroach appears from under her cot. Its feelers probe the air. Its body glows black, as if it has come to her from the darkest hole of hell. She tries to smash the demon with her Sexton book, but it vanishes beneath her bed. She shoves the bed aside, and there it is. She flattens it with her bare foot but it doesn't die. Sister Madeline watches the cockroach struggle. It drags its flattened body across the floor. It flips onto its back. Legs reach out. Feelers probe for something out there. Sister Madeline's eyes well with tears of joy. She feels God's presence once again.

> even the least
> persist in their quest
> for acceptance

Charlie's Stories

Last week Charlie left all his golf clubs and three decades of threadbare stories strewn about the course. Took them a day to clean up the mess and four caddie carts to bring it back. They dumped his clubs and his dreary life in our front yard. I wasn't cleaning that mess up. And Charlie, empty vessel that he was, just looked up and said, "Huh?" A week later someone had taken his clubs. Unfortunately, his stories still cluttered the front yard. So, dutiful as I am, I swept them up and dumped them in the big green container in the alley. All but that one about that wonderful Christmas Eve when we strolled along the beach chasing the waves in and out. I put it on the coffee table. Charlie didn't recognize it at first, then he looked up at me and smiled. What can I say? Sap that I am, I bent over and kissed his story-telling lips.

in drought
a single drop of water
becomes sacred

Misery

Hackmuth feels especially miserable today. Sure—kidneys, prostate, a recurrent carbuncle—that kind of thing. But this is more an existential gloom, an aura of meaninglessness and despair which puts him in a class by himself. Every day is the same. First, he tries to pee while staring at the broken tile between his feet. Next, he looks at himself in the mirror long enough to make sure he's more miserable than he was yesterday. Then he goes to The Bread and Butter Café for coffee with Fontes, a man he doesn't like very much. They play *How's Your This and How's Your That,* followed by a sinister round of *How the World Is Falling Apart.* Hackmuth always wins.

On his way to the park, he forces himself to smile at a few street people—insane ones, homeless ones, jerky-legged ones. If they smile back, he takes this to mean he's more miserable than they are. Their smiles, along with the stench of garbage and the fact that his shoes hurt his swollen feet, make his day almost perfect.

At the park Hackmuth visits Dog, a grizzled, near-dead canine with bad hips who lives by the mossy water faucet. He takes off a shoe and tosses it a few feet from Dog's nose. Dog stares at it, then manages to push himself up and drag over to the shoe. He brings it back to Hackmuth, wags his tail a couple of times, and returns to his faucet where he takes a lick or two and lies down. The wagging tells Hackmuth he's still more miserable than Dog.

The days go on like this, one after another. And every night Hackmuth goes to bed feeling fulfilled, happy to know that he is still the most miserable man in the world.

> slept-in body
> the scent of coffee
> a sense of purpose

American Self-Storage

Joe Fontes doesn't understand why he did it. Paid a year in advance to rent the smallest space available at American Self-Storage. As a young man he had imagined a small shrine to himself, a modest remembrance of his good and compassionate life. For a year now, his shrine has been a tiny room where he's stored the few things he lacked the courage to throw away: a few books and dusty manuscripts, an old percolator with no insides, the rusty frying pan that survived his first marriage, two cigars still in their wrapping, and a shoebox of outdated coupons that a woman named Leona gave him one evening in a bar. He could still hear her drunken laughter when she said she wouldn't need them, that she didn't make enough in tips to use them. "And besides," she said, "there's this cancer."

Fontes puts his stuff from the storage locker into a cardboard box and turns in the key. He writes FOR FREE on the box, takes it to The Bread and Butter Café on 4th Avenue, and hunkers down to wait. When someone pauses to look, he says, "Take it. It's yours." Eventually, a bum takes everything but the coupons. Fontes sorts through them, imagining what his life might have been—a doll and dollhouse on sale for his daughter, a Lazy Boy recliner, two bags of Lay's potato chips for the price of one, a lawn chair he could be sitting in right now while eating those chips....

He asks a passer-by for the time. The evening meal and prayer service at the Salvation Army will begin in ten minutes. Fontes tucks Leona's box of coupons under his arm, walks north on 4th, and turns west on Speedway.

sunset:
the day falling away
from untold stories

✧

Hackmuth's Sitting

You may not wonder why, but Hackmuth sits a lot. He sits on a park bench and stares at yesterday's newspaper. He sits and counts pigeons. He sits in front of a mirror and pretends the guy across from him is his inferior. He sits on the Salvation Army cot and counts his food stamps. Long ago, he joined sit-ins against the Vietnam War, back before the U.S. decided that wars were less messy when they relied on mercenaries. Now, he sits next to the dumpster in the alley on 4th Avenue with his neighbor, Fontes, a Vietnam vet. They smoke hand-rolled cigarettes and drink cheap wine. Fontes has no rocking chair, but he rocks a lot. Hackmuth rocks with him, considers it a gesture of solidarity. This week he sat in three coffee shops, a dozen or so bus stops, and four libraries. He has to keep moving, or they ask him to leave. When he has an extra dollar, he'll nurse a beer at a cheap bar. If you ask him, he'll tell you nothing comes of his sitting, no special wisdom, no flashes of understanding. But he won't tell you that he spends a lot of sit-time thinking about when he and his brother jumped up and down in the backseat of their father's car until the springs broke.

after his school burned
to cinders, he built
a book of blank pages

Walking Past

I want to sit beside that man in the threadbare coat, the one who sleeps curled up in the entryway. I want to offer a nod of acknowledgment to the vet with one arm and half-a-face. I want to know the name of the child who breathes the heavy air of a garbage can. I want to see those who are here and nowhere. I want to give this moment what it's asking for, at least a downward glance of compassion. But my eyes see through them and beyond, to the carnival on the hill.

on well-lit streets
hope for love lingers
even in neon shadows

Almost Home

She lives alone now that her husband is dead. But she's pleased that she's still allowed to drive. Tonight she's going home later than usual, but on a familiar road. The sun has set. Rows of white headlights and red tail-lights snake through the streets, some advancing, others retreating. She feels herself slipping into the murky soup of the night. She is lost and no one knows. Neon signs flash and spiral, invite her to BOWL AND RECEIVE FREE SHOES. TWO-FOR-ONE-SUSHI. ROMANTIC CRUISE. FUN WITH RUM. FURNITURE FOR NEWLYWEDS. FREE CHECKING. THREE DOLLAR BUDS. ALL NUDE DANCERS. URGENT CARE. Colors swirl, lights flash, engines roar. She is afraid and no one knows. She sees her street, turns left, then turns left again, into the third driveway. She stops her engine, walks bravely into her house and locks the door. She's at home. But not quite.

a moonless night
clouds of bats move
one darkness into another

Together Forty Years

Back then neither expected their lives to change that much, those times of bikinis, clear skies, and wild nights redolent with the scent of coconut oil. Now, forty years later, they lie in bed breathing air infused with Vicks and Bengay. She turns the last page of her most recent mystery, sighs, and places the book on the stack of other mysteries beside the bed. He watches a rerun of a soccer game he has seen before. It's between two countries he has never heard of, and he knows it will end in a zero-to-zero tie.

They don't talk as much these days. Their conversations have become codes uttered in hushed tones: *How'd you sleep? Bathroom at 3:52 again. Dinner? Meatloaf. Gravy? Change your t-shirt. Back? Pain moved to my hip. Nose? Still stuffy. Do you know you're wearing only one slipper? Yup.* And here they are, venerable old friends who have washed, folded, and put away four decades. Their pinkies touch. *Sleep well*, she says. Her eloquent sadness still moves him. *You too*, he says.

clouds in the distance
backlit pink by morning sun
darkness born of light

Hackmuth's Mannequin Dream

In Macy's he admires a mannequin. She resembles the woman on the billboard advertising the casino. She cares for him. He can feel it. For once it doesn't matter that he's knobby and stooped. He likes her too, her aloof air, the fact that her feet don't quite touch the floor. Perfect calves, long legs, trim hips. Then he's running, hobbling really, with her in his arms. A security guard cuts him off. He reverses direction and bumps her head on a Revlon cosmetics showcase. Her head falls off. Hackmuth stumbles up the escalator to the second floor. They pause long enough to admire small appliances, microwaves, silverware. He ducks into the men's room, sits hunched in a stall, with her on his lap, lovely, unruffled, long pointy fingers, headless. The guard is checking the stalls. Hackmuth holds her tighter and asks her to marry him. *But I'm not real*, she says. *Doesn't matter*, he says. *We can live in Iowa.* The guard rattles the door, demands they open up. Hackmuth strokes her smooth shoulders, reassures her that having a head doesn't matter. And that's when he wakes up, holding his pillow, alone and in love.

even a splinter
of moon reveals the landscape:
a radiant face

Heart Beans

At a restaurant called Pita Jungle, I'm eating a dish called One Thousand Beans. I'm trying to eat less fat and to take better care of my heart. And while I'm eating my beans, I overhear words from a man and woman in the next booth, words like *love, hate, disgust, guilt, best friends, have to stop, can't.* Then the man stops whispering and says in a clear voice, *How much time do we have left anyway?* A few seconds pass, and she starts to cry, not bawl but sniffle. How could she answer that question? Who could?

> every heart knows
> whatever happens later
> someone once loved it

And I can't help thinking about some terrible things I have done with wives and best friends and how, if I had it to do over again, I wouldn't change anything. Now, they're holding hands across the table, eyes locked in pain, sincerity, and love. And I'm eating my One Thousand Beans and thinking about love and how it might be the most important reason for my heart to survive. Maybe I will live one day longer or even one more minute for every bean I'm eating. And as these moments of insight so often go, I'm also thinking how hard it is to avoid fat and just eat beans.

Marriage, Scrabble, and LSD

Our romance started to wear thin when she took up Scrabble and LSD. Within a year she became a Scrabble champion averaging over 500 points despite words like *crucifix* that looked to her like mating snakes. I became her practice partner, and over a period of nine years, even though she often saw my hair on fire or a ferret boring its way into my ear, she won every game. Near the end she began to form words that were anagrams of MARRIAGE, words like MAR, RAGE, AGE, GRIM, RAM, and MIRAGE. On the last day we were together, I was cooking pork chops with a can of Campbell's mushroom soup, when she stormed into the kitchen, made a throaty, gagging sound, and screamed, "You're poisoning me, you...*aconite!*" After she left I looked the word up. *Aconite*: a seven-letter word meaning, a poisonous plant from the buttercup family.

marriage: a baseball field of snow—
the pitcher flings a snowball
it explodes on the bat
the runner on first looks around
to review his options

The Afterlife

For twenty years I had a season ticket, last seat at the end of row 29. In time, I knew everyone in my row. We screamed and high-fived with every basket and never doubted this would last forever. Then, Harriet Fisher had a stroke. Paul Fletcher had a heart attack. Meg Malone got hit while jaywalking. And Charlie Goucher, a laugher who sat next to me, was diagnosed with throat cancer. The last word I heard him say was *curable.* Before long, all the seats in row 29 except mine were occupied by strangers. They came late and left early. They said things like, *What's a free throw?* and when the score was tied with only six seconds left, they talked about cruises they'd taken. An obese adolescent sat in Charlie Goucher's seat. He ate hot dogs and yelled at inappropriate times. He knew nothing about the game, and he kept hogging the armrest. My desire to renew my ticket faded. This season I watch the games on TV with the sound off. But the game isn't the same. It lacks subtlety. I hardly recognize it.

> when the choir sings
> in perfect harmony
> death becomes an illusion

After I Didn't Die

and flunked out of hospice, it occurred to me that I had never owned a lava lamp. I wanted one and soon. I checked e-Bay. Nothing. But Amazon had dozens, all different colors and shapes. A silver one with blue water and yellow lava blobs arrived two days later. Now, I'm sitting on my bed watching my lamp. No gusto here, no driving ambition, just those slow-moving yellow blobs rising, sinking, moving up and down, softly colliding, changing shapes. And I can smell patchouli oil and weed, and the Beatles are singing "Yellow Submarine." I take a big brown pill and swallow. I cross my left leg over my right one, take it back, and cross it again. Amazing how the body moves—sliding, rising, sinking, always changing. Even these fingers that hold a glass of water. I like looking at them. Then I hear Peg Duncan's laughter that time at the drive-in movie when her skirt got stuck in my zipper. She's been dead for twenty years and I still keep the gift certificate she gave me for Barnes and Noble. I'll never cash it. I'm remembering her and watching that lava lamp. I'm big-eyed and smiling because I'm still here and the things that make most sense are those yellow bubbles floating in that womb of blue water.

from now on
every gesture, one of love
it's all clear profit

"I Feel Good"

Awoke this morning and thought of James Brown. Thirty years have passed since I heard his biggest hit. Found the old 33 rpm in my collection and put it on. It came straight at me like a tornado: *OWWWW, I FEEL GOOD, dada, dada-ditty-dum.* My rusty soul motor sputtered, then took off. My legs made some moves. My arms flapped. My hips squiggled. I did a slick side-slide and jigged down the back steps. I detached my complaining and compromising head, and lobbed it over my neighbor's fence. Sarah was hanging her laundry at the time. "Get that thing out of here," she said. *OWWWW,* my head said as my body snaked through the back hedge and freewheeled down the alley while Sarah—arms outstretched—chased me and called, "Come back, Dan. You forgot your head."

> trapped in an ice cave
> the devout philosopher
> dies from frost bite

Making a Deal with God

You have to understand, God. After I didn't die, I really believed I'd been chosen, that I was an angel. My ecstatic insights astonished me. I loved everyone. I *was* love. I loved toads and sand and bark on trees. I had to tell the world about Your gifts. Then suddenly my insights vanished like a flock of pigeons.

For a while I faked it—lifted lines from Gibran, Mother Theresa, and Moses. But I came to suspect they faked it too. Gibran died bitter and disillusioned. Mother Theresa, wracked with doubt, faked her faith all those years. And I suspect all that *loving your neighbor* and *not coveting other's wives* wasn't really Yours, just the delusions of a demented old man who had no teeth and still liked to bite.

I think I understand now. The unknowable is Your realm, and You get upset when we humans dare to think we know and comprehend Your nature. I understand that a kind of earned ignorance is the best we can hope for—not stupidity, just a golden question mark that comes after years of trying to make sense of things. I understand that finally embracing the gift of not-knowing is true grace.

So I'm back to being human—doing my laundry, eating my Cheerios, judging others, hating most politicians, coveting wives—the whole human disaster. So, God, should You exist, even in ways that are beyond comprehension, here's my proposal: Grant me a few more years of being me, and I'll stay on my side of the fence—no more ecstatic insights, no more thinking I actually know something. Hey, I'd be willing to consider a counterproposal. But that's not going to happen, is it? See, I get it.

evening sea
a single gull at low tide
still fishing

✧

My Big Brown Cup

I'm in my office now trying to write and I miss my old brown coffee cup. I've been with it longer than I've been with my wife. I'm thinking she threw it away. The wimpy yellow one she gave me as a replacement doesn't work. The big brown one had words in it. I'd drink a cup and the words flowed out of my pencil so fast the paper would sizzle. But the yellow one is illiterate and lazy. It sits around all day, yappy happy yellow, and stares at a blank page as if it were a mine field. I need my gruff brown cup. I should confront my wife nose-to-nose and force her to tell me what she did with it. I'm thinking this when she walks in, plops down on my sofa, looks at the empty-headed bereft version of me, and says, "I found that brown cup of yours. Do you still want it?"

"Yes," I say, "I love that cup." I manage to suppress my urge to say, *Ah ha, guilty, just as I thought.* My wife raises an eyebrow. Then I add, "I love you too." The room is quiet now. Words are leaping around like swarming locusts. It's true, I love my wife, I really do. But my big brown cup makes all love possible.

old dogs stay in their yards
long after the fence has fallen
it's not fear but faith

Problems

You sit on the sofa in your old red robe, reading a book. From all appearances you have no problems. I sit across from you, worrying about my rheumatism problem, my money problem, my blood-thinner problem, my need-to-be-adored problem, my Republican problem, my gimpy-right-leg problem, my world-overpopulation problem, my what's-the-meaning-of-all-this problem—and my too-many-problems problem.

>   the boat lists, sails ripped
>   loaded with heroes but none
>   know what to do

It begins to snow again. You glance at the falling flakes, look at the fireplace and then at me. You study my face as if you aren't sure who I am. Then you smile. The smile of a child at a candy store who points and says, "I'll take that one." You pull your legs up under yourself and begin reading again. If this moment were a fish, it would be too small to keep. But today, I don't have a problem with that.

Happy Valley Conversion

David and Norma Poindexter of the luxury Cavalier double-wide are coming to tell Mabel all the ways she has violated Happy Valley Neighborhood Association's Covenant. Only ten minutes to prepare herself for the flogging. Mabel can't stand them: David with his bolo tie, gooey black hair, and his big just-got-my-teeth-whitened smile. Norma with her perfect size-twenty dress, carefully tossed blond hair, and pouty lips. They make Mabel in her used single-wide Fleetwood feel six years old. She's worried that her potted pansies are the wrong color. She tries to remember if she picked that weed by the water meter. Did she wipe the bird poop off the mail box? The doorbell rings. She stuffs a pizza box into the trash and takes a swipe at the TV screen with her skirt. Suddenly she feels bilious. She wants a Stouffer's bacon mac-and-cheese dinner. David and Norma don't know that she was once a supervisor at Target and won three Employee of the Month awards. She bites her lower lip and opens the door, ready to vow to do better. But David and Norma are all huggy and kissy. Who wouldn't admire David's Happy Valley smile and Norma's proud hair? And when David asks her if she could possibly consent to serve on the Covenant Committee, Mabel says, "Really? But why me?" And Norma says, "Because you are you, Mabel, so friendly and conscientious." And Mabel says, "I'd be honored and humbled." They hug, have coffee, then hug again, and Mabel, on the verge of tears, asks if they might have an extra copy of the Covenant.

to the seeker
even the scent of incense
makes him fall to his knees

Ellie's Stubborn Spirit

"Tinker Bells and Sunflowers." That's the name of the wallpaper Ellie found in *Good Housekeeping*. She'd never papered anything before. But she was the most stubborn-spirited woman Owen had ever known. She dove in and when she finished, the kitchen walls were covered—Tinker Bells with deformed legs, sunflowers with broken stems. His first thought was, *Enough. I've had it. I'm divorcing Ellie and marrying Marlene Miller.* She was the organ player at the church. Compliant to a fault. Ellie could keep everything except his drift-wood pole lamp and his collection of meat thermometers.

Just then, she came in wearing her robe and that morning scowl of hers. She looked at her wallpaper job, put her fists on her hips, and said, "There needs to be a magazine called *Bad Housekeeping*. I'd win the house of the year award." She tilted her head this way and that. "But those wrinkles," she said. "You stay with them long enough and you realize they make a statement, together, don't you think?"

Owen asked if she was considering redoing it. "Nope," she said. She opened the refrigerator and spooned out some leftover broccoli-and-chicken casserole. He watched her chew and smile at the same time, and remembered the time she invented a salve for removing his wart. The wart had disappeared overnight, but he didn't think it was Ellie's salve that did it. What he thought was, she put some of her will into that salve and the wart just gave up.

somewhere
a horsefly is bringing
a herd to its knees

✧

The Musician's Bible

I sat the thick book down in front of my wife. She was still working on her first cup of coffee, and I could almost hear her wishing me away. "Found it in the garage," I said. "Haven't seen one of these for thirty years. They're called fake books. You know, as in 'make it up, improvise,' but we call them The Bible. A thousand tunes arranged alphabetically with basic chords and unadorned melodies. A tune for any occasion, from 'All of Me' to 'Zip-a-Dee-Doo-Dah.' Not a real Bible though—no credo, no guilt, no tune claiming to be the right one. You play it as you feel it, sad one day, happy the next. Thirty-two measures to find your soul."

My wife peered over the rims of her glasses. I sang a bluesy version of "All of Me," did a little shimmy and extended the ending—*Why not take all*, I said, *why not take all...of...me?* My wife said, "It's too early for this."

"Check this one out," I said, and crooned a snappy version of "Cheek to Cheek," blasted out a ONE MORE TIME extended coda, and gave her a big smooch on the lips. "Well?" I said, arms spread. She was defenseless. All she could manage was, "Amen."

he picks up his horn
hears his heart whisper
"recess"

Like That

Mike tells it like this: "We'd played together for nine years before it happened. Then one night Tommy pushed the bass just a little ahead. I jumped on-board and rode high over that beat, Gene found the mood on guitar, Gil played a simple counterpoint, and Connie brought it together on drums. So tight, it was almost scary. Never felt anything like that, not even close."

In the years that followed, Gene committed suicide, Connie died of leukemia, Gil became a carpenter and lost two fingers, Tommy died of an overdose, and Mike, in his eighties, is now a street musician on Shattuck Avenue in Berkeley. He doesn't remember much about the others. "We didn't talk much," he says. "But that night. It was something." He points to some birds lined up on a power line equidistant apart. He watches as all of them lift off at once and soar as if each bird is a part of the same being. "Like that," Mike says. "Like that."

<blockquote>
hummingbirds hover
in one place
yet so passionately
</blockquote>

Last Call

for Dan Wolfe
February 1954–October 2015

You're making a life. You're hoisting something heavy. You've memorized the changes. You've practiced all the scales, listened to all the experts. You've got the beat down. You know it's three choruses of thirty-two bars and you fill them with ease. And you're thinking, *I got this down.* Then the drummer throws the beat or the piano player calls a different tune or worse yet, no one shows up to listen. And you are making something beautiful, something that soars out of you like a bird in flight, and no one hears it except the bartender who's tone deaf or the guy who stumbles in late looking for a cowboy joint down the street. Suddenly you're playing the last set and you are trying so hard to keep it clean and beautiful that you feel tears squeezing from the corners of your eyes. You are trying not to think about how roses can't grow on cement, and maybe about some of the wrong notes you've played, when the bartender flicks the lights for last call and you go home, have a beer, eat a bologna and cheese sandwich, brush your teeth, look for the gun buried at the bottom of your sock drawer—and then you quietly drive into the woods and shoot yourself in the head.

early morning
ice-cream truck parked
on an empty street

The Cabinet Maker

He is contained in a cocoon of soft silence as he applies the last stroke of varnish to the table and leans in for a closer look. For a moment the table, he himself, his reflection, and every wood chip scattered about his floor are contained in a single existence. And in the stillness, he ceases to exist.

rain vista
falling leaves
winging through time

Holding Death Close

The vet asked if I wanted to hold my cat while the injection took effect. I knew she didn't like being held, but I held her anyway. A few seconds passed. "She's purring," I said. The vet said that cats often purr when they're dying. Then she was gone. The vet told me to take as long as I needed and left. I sat on a steel bench holding my cat. She was so still. She had never been this still. It was a stillness like I'd never felt, a stillness that says so much and reveals so little.

> broken wind chimes
> no calming melodies
> wind waits to be heard

The Three-Legged Dog

A rusted-out car swayed precariously at the edge of a bluff above the city dump. That old car was the dog's home. She hunkered down in the back seat when men came in their pickups to drink beer and shoot rats. Sometimes she'd peek out and cock her head as if she were considering leaving but couldn't figure out where a beat-up three-legged dog like her could go.

One day the men stood beside their pickups at the bottom of the hill and shot up at her car. "Kill her," one yelled. "Put her out of her misery!" another shrieked. They laughed as their bullets pinged off rocks and clunked into the car's hood. One grazed the dog's ear. But this time she didn't hide in the back seat. She sat in the driver's seat, paws on the steering wheel as the car rocked forward then broke loose and rolled down the bluff.

It picked up speed, catapulted over a boulder, and slammed into one of the pickups. And suddenly, except for the squawk of a few gulls, the dump was silent. The men looked at the dented pickup. One poked the dog with his gun barrel to make sure she was dead. That night when the moon was out and the dump was sizzling with ferment, the three-legged dog was still in the driver's seat.

safe now in the woods
a wounded deer slumps and falls
and dies on its own terms

Prayers

When Ted was sacked from his job at Pella Windows, he was afraid to tell his wife. He drove all day on the back roads of Iowa and found himself in a small town surrounded by cornstalks and blowing hot dust. He parked in front of a place with a Budweiser sign, walked up some wooden steps, pulled his hoodie over his head, and went in. The screen door slapped behind him. Nobody looked up. Three old men sat in a dusty corner as if they had finally mastered the art of waiting. One was telling a story about a horse that couldn't swim, how he had watched that horse flail about in the middle of a river until it drowned.

silence in a packed church
someone coughs
everyone wants to

A woman, not old but worn out, stood behind the bar, arms braced. "Welcome to the end of the road," she said. "It ain't the classiest of places but it's all you got." Ted ordered a draft. Next to the cash register was a religious candle of some sort. He asked the woman if she was Catholic. "Nope," she said. "I worship at the shrine of Jim Beam." She said the candle belonged to her son. She showed Ted a prayer that was inscribed on the candle. "It's called *Prayer to the Virgin Mary as the Untier of Knots*," she said. "He prayed that prayer right up to his last amen." Ted told her that he had a few knots that needed untying. She held out the candle. "Take it. It's yours," she said. "Maybe my boy pushed it right up to the edge. Maybe one more prayer will do it."

the slot machine whirls
two cherries and a horseshoe
he drops another coin

When Ted left, the old man was telling his horse story again like no one had heard it before. Outside, he put the candle on the seat, started the engine, and headed home. He would call his wife when he got in range.

heads bowed everywhere
looking for answers
on their smart phones

Empathy

At the first break the drummer sits between Johnny and Midge, and Johnny says to me, "Give the kid a drink, Frank. It'll help him feel better about himself." So I draw a draft and Johnny says, "My eyes are welling for this kid, Frank. It's called empathy. You ever hear of empathy, Frank? That's what I'm feeling. I feel your pain, kid. Hey, not everyone has rhythm. It's all right. Maybe the 6th Army Marching band—"

Midge pipes up, "Hey, lay off the kid, you old fart." And Johnny says, "What do you mean, lay off. I'm trying to help him." Midge gives Johnny the finger and says, "Help this, ass hole." And Johnny who can't let go of nothing comes off with this brilliant retort: "Yeah, up yours, Midge." But he doesn't stop there. He says in this loud voice, "I don't like being cruel, especially to women, but nobody, I mean nobody can stand up to Johnny Gold when he's on, and I AM ON. Give me another Scotch, Frank."

The drummer ain't said nothing. He just walks back to the bandstand. Then, boom: the bass player starts a line, and the drummer kicks in with the snare and high hat, then the piano guy does this bluesy riff, and it sounds pretty good. They're swinging, and Johnny says real loud over the music. "It feels so good to help this kid out, maybe I even saved him from suicide. This is me, you know, I try to do something kind for someone at least once a day."

a narcissist
swaggers past wild plums roadside
feels a surge of pride

Olives for Antonya Nelson

Larry moved to a guest house near the university to write his novel for his MFA degree. His landlord told him that a writer by the name of Antonya Nelson had lived there previously. "My God," Larry said. "She's incredible. She's fantastic." He didn't say that he loved Antonya, seriously loved her, that he dreamed of meeting her someday. But at least he had a plot for his novel now: *handsome young writer moves into the former residence of a sex-crazed famous writer. One day there's a knock,* etc.

Larry wrote with focus and determination. It was good, really good. And while he wrote, he imagined Antonya behind him, reading each word, breathing heavily, even gasping at times, occasionally hooking a strand of hair over her ear, bringing out her intelligent and cruel authorial whip when Larry left a modifier dangling.

creativity
like the blues—a delicious
three-chord misery

Then Antonya came to town for a reading. Larry bought a meet-the-author ticket. There she was—raked-back hair, leather skirt, black stockings, heels with silver-studded toes. But her admirers surrounded her. How could he possibly make an impression? An idea came to him. He stuck black olives on four of his fingertips, held his hand high in the air, and worked his way through the crowd. *Excuse me, pardon me, olives, Antonya has requested olives.* And there he was, his olive-fingers in front of her face. His knees turned to water. The only thing he could think to say was, "Olive?"

Antonya said, "No, thank you" and turned to talk to a woman who had a question about dialogue. Larry ate the olives, left the party, and drove back to his guest house. That night as he occupied the space formerly occupied by Antonya's bed, he vowed celibacy, and decided that for the rest of his life, he'd bathe in the rivers of poetry.

in severe drought
the olive tree's only prayer:
its dry limbs

On Saying *I Love You*

At sunrise I'm scrubbing the burnt drippings from the pan that I used for the roast chicken last night. And I'm thinking about when you sat there at the counter long ago, watching me roast a different chicken while you sipped retsina.

Was it a Greek chicken? I remember taking it out of the oven, its crisp skin, the scents of rosemary and garlic, the thick crust of oregano. I stood there in my chef's apron and watched you eat in great hungry mouthfuls. And I remember when you swallowed you applauded and said I must write an erotic cookbook.

And just as I'm thinking how sometimes saying *I love you* isn't enough, you walk in, bundled in your terrycloth robe, hug me from behind, and say *I love you*. My eyes mist up. I want to say, *I need to tell you something. Everything—this leftover chicken, this empty bottle, this pan, all those years of lemon scents and oregano, the two of us—they are the breath of the same body, the beat of the same heart, the laughter of the same god.* But instead, I put the pan in the drying rack and say, *I love you too.*

> when Eve bit the apple
> the gates of paradise opened
> and poetry was invented

Paradise Lost

The night before the exam, I had confidence that I could ace it. Took Dexedrine. Intended to speed-read the entire book. But I couldn't get past the first page. It was like ten thousand foreign words were running around a field, lurching and flinging themselves against one another. I asked my roommate what *Paradise Lost* is about. He said, "It's like, you know, this guy who finds a wallet stuffed with money and loses it."

So, I filled three blue books trying to show how *Paradise Lost* is relevant to contemporary society. I wrote about how life is a continuous cycle of hope and loss, of paradises gained and paradises lost—life, love, faith, muscles, health, how country music and the blues give voice to loss. Opera too. I wrote about the wallet guy, about this beautiful girl I saw last week who had lost a leg. I wrote about how I was cut from my high school baseball team, my father who never played catch with me, the ant colony I wiped out with poisonous pellets, Vietnam, Iraq, Hiroshima, hair…I couldn't stop.

I flunked. "Interesting," my prof scrawled across the top. "But what does this have to do with the book?" Of course, I didn't know. Nor did I care. All I could think of was those poor ants feasting on my poison.

threadbare tires
the bus to Shangri-La must cross
rivers lined with spikes

✧

Summer Night-Sounds of Tucson

Of course coyotes, always coyotes, and the shrill barks of small dogs that guide these starving, wild ones to their midnight meals. The muffled moans of illegals as they make their way across razor-edged rocks. The snorts of javelinas chewing a cactus for a drop of water. The snores of passed-out drunk faux-cowboys lying face-down on searing parking-lot asphalt. And the old ones who are counting ticks of clocks and heart monitors while waiting for the first sounds of morning traffic. Piercing sounds of sirens and throbs of helicopter blades that no longer produce fear, but numbed annoyance. Muffled weeping everywhere while a dozen Mexican radio stations compete with broken-throated songs of great love and brassy out-of-tune polkas. And the painful whimpers of someone's mother being helped downstairs to the bathroom while her little red-eyed dog watches and barks its concern. And closer now, hunched down on all fours, listening to its barks, the coyotes alert and hungry. Always the coyotes.

an axe of sunlight
splits the night
tennis players volley
golfers tee off
paradise reclaimed

Sam Snyder's Puzzlement

For twenty years he taught high school English. For five days a week, six hours a day he battled acne-covered zombies with unquestionably bad hygiene. He lost every time. While attending a Zen retreat, he was whacked several times by the teacher with an "awakening stick." And for a while Sam considered buying a cattle prod to use in a similar way on his dimwits.

> a pound of copper
> surrounded by a mountain
> of stony waste

Although he was haunted by hopelessness, Sam was also a gentle man who loved literature. When he tried to teach his cretins about *Huck Finn* or *The Old Man and the Sea*, Marilyn Fletcher wrote crude notes to Frank Bauer who made lewd tongue-gestures and jabbed Mike Moore who was sleeping off a hangover. Carol Lee combed Stan Ashbury's greasy hair while Stan maintained an LSD-induced, cow-eyed look of seeing God. And all the while Francine Butts, a loner, picked at a wart and drooled. All this in a tempest of nose-picking, giggling, zit-squeezing, and random farting.

> Jesus walked on water
> Armstrong walked on the moon
> somewhere a mind changed

Years later, Marilyn Fletcher became a champion for defeating world hunger. Mike Moore served as defense lawyer for Stan Ashbury who choked his wife Carol Lee to death with the A-string from his guitar. Before her death, Carol Lee was anchor on the evening news. Frank Bauer of lewd-gesture fame now owns a McDonald's franchise and, picking and drooling her way to a PhD, Francine Butts became an English teacher. More puzzling to Sam is the fact that he occasionally gets notes from them, thanking him for all he did to inspire them. Last week Stan Ashbury wrote and thanked Sam for introducing him to great literature. He said he had only twenty-seven more years to serve.

every board, warped
every nail, bent
yet the house is livable

Self-Help

My friend, Stella Ratliff, reads self-help books. Last Tuesday we met for coffee and bagels. Stella said I seemed happy. She was surprised because I'm usually morose. I told her that I dreamed about getting even with Jeff Winkler, a kid in seventh grade who stole Jenny Norwood away from me. "In my dream," I said, "I slaughtered ole Jeffrey in a game of badminton. Every overhand was a birdie drilled straight at his chest. And that's why I'm happy." Stella tells me that everything in my dream represents a different part of me, that I am simultaneously myself, Jeff, Jenny, and the birdie. She said my dream was telling me that I have stolen a part of myself from me and am getting even with me by attacking my own heart with a frightened bird-like part of me. I asked, what was the part I stole? She said, "Chest? Heart? Don't you get it? It's your ability to love."

So I asked, "Then why did I wake up happy?" And she said that dreams are the best things we have for punishing ourselves for our own pathologies. My mind could not process this. Stella was buttering her bagel when the man at the next table spilled hot coffee all over his lap. Stella smiled a knowing little smile and said, "See? Need I say more?"

> all day miners bore
> holes and search through sludge before
> they quit to drink beer

✧

Raymond's Epiphany

Dr. Sally Sperling set out to prove that, when it comes to sex, male rats never learn. Raymond was her research assistant. His job was to match female rats in heat with one of twenty males—each with his own roomy cage, a continuous supply of food and water, and a floor covered with three inches of clean sawdust. All night, every night, Raymond videotaped each male's mating behavior. Dr. Sperling was right. The sexual behavior of the male hooded rat wasn't pretty. It consisted mainly of wild pursuit, leaping, groping, pouncing, and pounding. Terrified females scurried around the sides of the cages, defecated and urinated, engaged in frantic grooming, and fought viciously when their suitors attempted to copulate. "Sex is a high anxiety, risky business," Dr. Sperling said. This corresponded with Raymond's limited experience.

Then one evening a female savagely killed one of the males, and Dr. Sperling—perhaps as a cruel joke or with idle curiosity—replaced the dead male with a refugee from a brain-lesion experiment. She called him Mr. Big because he weighed the equivalent of a three-hundred-pound human. He resembled a furry white doily with two eyes and a pink nose in the middle. Dr. Sperling chuckled. "No chance, Mr. Big," she said.

> on cloudy days too
> doesn't the sunflower turn
> toward the sun

One night after Mr. Big had faced repeated and humiliating failures, he modified his approach. When Raymond placed a female in his cage, instead of leaping and pouncing, Mr. Big sat in his corner gazing out while his visitor familiarized herself with her new surroundings. Raymond noted that he must be giving up. Mr. Big hardly noticed when she sampled his chow and licked his water bottle. He looked away when she rooted in his sawdust.

After a while Mr. Big lumbered to the center of his sawdust bed and focused his pink gaze on the upper regions of his cage. His visitor approached. She sniffed his front parts, quivered slightly, and nuzzled his hind parts. At that point Mr. Big pulled out a poem he had written for the occasion. And there before his nose, his lover raised her hind parts and settled into a receptive position. The rest is private, of course, but quite moving. A soft devastation.

Raymond reported all this to Dr. Sperling, but she didn't believe him and blamed it on his sleep deprivation. She excluded Mr. Big from the study because he was too fat and brain-damaged. So Raymond took Mr. Big home, where they wrote poetry together. Whenever Raymond became discouraged, Mr. Big assured him that someday someone would come along that he could show just how good love can be.

table set, cheeks flushed
she waits on the balcony
watches the freeway
Gibran on the coffee table
stiletto in the planter

The Hyperbolist

under the scorching sun
a man scuttles on tiptoes
between plots of shade

I spent most of my life addicted to the pursuit of truth, an affliction that almost destroyed me. I devoured world religions, history, and statistics; sat Zen meditation and suffered sweat lodges; read *The Fountainhead* and *Summerhill*; struggled with Ordinary Language Analysis; drank from the bitter cup of love with three wives; had a go at theoretical physics and music; tried skydiving, colonics, calisthenics, fire walking, tantric twosomes and moresomes, encounter groups, twelve Rolfing sessions, neuropsychology, existentialism, behaviorism, logical positivism, hedonism, atheism, asceticism, depth psychology, NASCAR, Iyangar, and *Dancing With the Stars*.

untenured faculty
forage academic minefields
feverishly picking
over dry bones, looking
for bite-size morsels of truth

I walked every path, looked under every stone, and in the end became a slave to subtlety, a restrained but very dull trivializer. My search for truth made me a listless, list-making snob, a self-righteous skeptic, a person who possessed all the attributes of those college professors who year after year manage to fool their students into believing they are alive. Finally, I escaped to poetry, to the world of fantasy and imagination. Surely this would give me some relief from my dreary search for truth. But after reading my first poem, my instructor said I must tell the truth, that my poem was filled with *hyperbole*. To me this seemed like a good thing. What was wrong with turning the common weeds of life into gigantic fields of orchids? Enough picking at the crusty scabs of this elusive thing called truth. And there, while I brooded over my failed poem, the spirit of excess entered me. I became a Hyperbolist.

> from the rain forest
> I borrowed a small clipping
> planted it in my back yard
> and now my place is a jungle
> populated by pygmies

I dedicated myself to filling the rest of my life with ballyhoo, exalted desire, exorbitant self-pity, wild and forbidden love, and unrestrained sensationalism. Today, *all* my weeping willows are giant oaks with limbs that embrace hucksterism. I tell my tales with unbridled amplification and shamelessly excessive lily-gilding. I boast of my achievements, proclaim loudest the most mundane, proudly parade my losses and choices that almost destroyed me. I turn all my molehills into mountains, attack dusty storms of truth with the waters of my imagination, brandish my sword in the name of intemperate celebration. I throw off the reins of propriety. I dance the dance of embellishment. I am addicted to blatant ornamentation and corpulent elaboration. For it's the garnish of excess that tastes so much sweeter than the truth-teller's gray meat. I worship the gods of exaggeration and believe with all my heart that facts always stand in the way of a well-told story.

> giant flesh-eating buzzards
> attacked me, yet I escaped—
> and no, they weren't gnats

One with Everything

Argon is the most prevalent gas on earth. It's everywhere. It's indestructible. It enters and leaves our bodies through our breath, and lasts forever. Every pant, huff, and cough ever made exist in you for all eternity. Your breath the first time you said, *I love you*, and all those times you laughed and cried and gasped for joy are still there. Every owl's *who*, every pig's squeal, and the last breath of every dying person are in you. And you are exhaling them into the universe, where they will be inhaled by all who will come after you.

look ahead
there you are
look behind
there you are still

You will forever contain the breath of warm whispers of love, the violent gestures of birth, the bellowing of every slaughtered cow, the collective hum of this struggling earth and heavens and everything on or in them. Breathe, and know that your breath contains everything that has laughed and wailed and howled throughout the eons. Yours is the same breath gulped by Jesus when he said, *Forgive them*, the same deep sigh released by Rilke when he finally wrote, *You must change your life*.

Your mother and father, Attila the Hun, Buddha, Rembrandt, and Shakespeare all exist in you. Every tree, bush, and microbe. Every hawk, every hammerhead shark, every hyena. All of history, all creativity and passion, all snarls of cruelty and hymns of joy live in you.

When you think of your death or of being alone, or when you consider the world a thousand years from now, remember this:

All that ever was lives on in you, and you will forever live in all eternity.

> falling leaf stirs the air
> ten thousand miles away
> and enters the world's soul

Three-Wheeler

Each afternoon when she peddled by on her three-wheeler tour of the neighborhood, she rang the little bell mounted on her handle bars and waved. She seemed happy. Franklyn wanted to be like her, a joyful elder riding a bicycle with an extra wheel, a confident man with a little bell to ring and others to wave to. But his happiness was more the two-wheel variety, rickety and wobbly. His life needed a third wheel. A significant other perhaps? No, he'd tried that enough times to know that *significance* is not often paired with *other*. A faith of sorts might be nice. But faith is so frequently served with a side sauce of optimism and hope, both of which he had a hard time digesting.

One day he stopped the old woman, and after some preliminary chatter about tire inflation and so on, he asked if her three-wheeler brought her happiness. She thought for a moment and said, "You really don't have to be happy to ride a three-wheeler. You just have to peddle." This made as much sense as anything else, so Franklyn bought one. The fact that his little bell was slightly louder than hers was entirely unintentional. Now, when they pass, Franklyn feels a kind of giddiness as he waves and rings his bell and peddles on.

lightning strike
the oak burns a week before
dropping its leaves

✧

Miracles

for Ted Kooser

Ted and I are drinking beer in the run-down Corner Bar in Garland, Nebraska, population, 210. Fran, the bartender, loses interest when I start giving Ted my take on miracles—the miracle that more of us aren't killed for tweeting when we drive; the miracle that on most days, the majority of us actually find something to eat and safe water to drink. Ted signals Fran for another round as I tell him what a miracle it is that terrorists haven't already set off a bomb at the Super Bowl.

When I pause, he holds up his bottle to the light and tells me about a beer bottle he saw in a burned-out highway ditch. "Tossed from a car," he says. "It had landed straight up, unbroken. Like a cat thrown off a roof that landed hard and stands dazzled in the sun, right side up." He takes a slug of beer. "Sort of a miracle," he says.

And Fran says, "Was that bottle over on Lakeside Road near the Holland bridge?" And Ted says, "Indeed it was."

"That's my bottle," Fran says. "I tossed it out over a week ago. Landed right side up, and still standing, eh?" She looks me in the eye. "Now that's a miracle."

perched on a post
raven waits for car and rabbit
to cross paths

The Radiance

I want to go on record about the radiant light reported by people who have almost died but came back to life. Speaking for myself, and not wanting to upset anybody's belief applecart, I wish to report that I have had a near-death experience and didn't see the light.

I was in an Italian restaurant and had just ordered linguine with clam sauce. Then suddenly, I was in a long hallway, no doors, dim lighting. At the end of the hall was a tiny figure of what appeared to be a dog wearing a sombrero. I walked toward it, and the figure came slowly toward me. But instead of growing larger as it got closer, it grew smaller. I was right. It was a dog wearing a sombrero, but by the time it sat in front of me it was only an inch tall and the sombrero was tiny. We looked at one another with mutual disappointment. I was disappointed that the dog was so small, that it did not talk or even bark, that it carried no message in its mouth, that its tail didn't wag, and that it was…a dog. We both turned and walked back to where we came from.

That's when I came back to life—in an ambulance on the way to the emergency room. The attendant said the waiter had put my linguine carbonara in a box to go. I told him I had ordered linguine with clam sauce. So I gave the carbonara to a nurse who said her dog would love it. Please enter this in the archives of near-death experiences.

always living
and always dying
we play with the dogs we're dealt

✧

End Matter

Life is no more than a dream—but don't wake me up.

—Yiddish proverb

A Special Note of Thanks

This book would not exist without the assistance, inspiration, loving support, creativity, careful eye, patience, hard work, and genuine caring of Clare MacQueen, founding editor and publisher of *KYSO Flash*. Thank you Clare for introducing me to haibun and for encouraging me to experiment with the form. Your good work inspires good work.

I also wish to thank poets Tom Speer, Jackie Newlove, Jan Smith, and Gerry Connally for their reading and critiques of many of the haibun in this collection.

—Dan Gilmore
Tucson, Arizona
April, 2016

Acknowledgments

Front-cover photograph of "Manifest Destiny" (Foot Fetish #67) appears with kind permission from the artist, Gwen Murphy.

Written works appear herein with permission from the author, Dan Gilmore. Of these 53 works, 38 were created especially for this collection, and 15 are reprints as indicated below.

"After I Didn't Die" was first published in the *KYSO Flash* online literary journal (Issue 3, Spring 2015), and is reprinted here from the author's chapbook of haibun stories, *Just Before Sleep* (KYSO Flash Press, 2015).

"After 9-11" and **"Big Boy"** were first published in *KYSO Flash* (Issue 4, Fall 2015).

"Hackmuth's Mannequin Dream," "Happiness," and **"I Feel Good"** are reprinted from *KYSO Flash* (Issue 5, Spring 2016).

"Lazarus Ponders His Resurrection" is adapted from the lineated poem "Lazarus and Me" in Dan Gilmore's *Love Takes a Bow* (Imago Press, 2010).

"Making a Deal with God" is adapted from a lineated poem with the same name in *Love Takes a Bow* (Imago Press, 2010).

"Misery" is adapted from "Faucet Dogs," a lineated poem in *Love Takes a Bow* (Imago Press, 2010).

"My Big Brown Cup" is from *KYSO Flash* (Issue 4, Fall 2015).

"New Shoes" is adapted from a lineated poem with the same name from Gilmore's *Panning for Gold* (Imago Press, 2014), and is reprinted here from his chapbook of haibun stories, *Just Before Sleep* (KYSO Flash Press, 2015).

"On Saying *I Love You*" and **"Prayers"** were first published in *KYSO Flash* (Issue 5, Spring 2016).

"The Afterlife" is adapted from "Season Tickets," a lineated poem in Dan Gilmore's *Season Tickets* (Pima Press, 2003).

"Visitation" was first published as a tribute featured in "Kowit's Korner" in *Serving House Journal* (Issue 14, Spring 2016).

Appendix: Alpha List of Works

28   After 9-11
42   After I Didn't Die
36   Almost Home
33   American Self-Storage
22   Beliefs
24   Big Boy
31   Charlie's Stories
30   Dark Angel
21   Early Religious Experiences
48   Ellie's Stubborn Spirit
57   Empathy
38   Hackmuth's Mannequin Dream
34   Hackmuth's Sitting
27   Happiness
47   Happy Valley Conversion
39   Heart Beans
53   Holding Death Close
43   "I Feel Good"
51   Last Call (*for Dan Wolfe*)
26   Lazarus Ponders His Resurrection
50   Like That
16   Looking for Something
44   Making a Deal with God
40   Marriage, Scrabble, and LSD [*]
73   Miracles (*for Ted Kooser*)
32   Misery
45   My Big Brown Cup
15   New Shoes
58   Olives for Antonya Nelson
25   On Easter Morning
60   On Saying *I Love You*
70   One with Everything
18   Overheard in Silverman's Deli, St. Paul, Minnesota
61   Paradise Lost

---

[*] Indicates tanka prose rather than haibun story, and contains one or more tanka (five-line poems) rather than haiku (three-line poems)

✧

Author's Bio

Dan Gilmore is the author of a novel, *A Howl for Mayflower* (Imago Press, 2006); a chapbook of haibun stories, *Just Before Sleep* (KYSO Flash, 2015); and three collections of poetry and monologues: *Season Tickets* (Pima Press, 2003), and *Love Takes a Bow* and *Panning for Gold* (Imago Press, 2010 and 2014, respectively). He has won the Raymond Carver Fiction Contest, the Martindale Fiction Award, and multiple Sandscript Awards for Short Stories. His poems have appeared in *Atlanta Review*, *San Diego Reader*, *Aethlon*, *Blue Collar Review*, *The Carolina Review*, *Sandscript*, *Loft and Range*, *KYSO Flash*, and *Serving House Journal*.

"Happiest Black White Man Alive," one of Gilmore's flash fictions, was nominated for a Pushcart Prize, and was chosen by Pulitzer-Prize-winning novelist Robert Olen Butler as among the top 55 stories for publication in *The Best Small Fictions 2015*.

In his time, Gilmore has been:

a fry cook,
a jazz musician,
a draft dodger,
a soldier,
an actor,
a minister in a Reno wedding chapel,
a psychologist,
a single parent of two children,
a college professor,
a dean, and
a consultant to business.

For additional biographical notes, photographs of the author, and information about his books, please visit his website:

http://dangilmorewrites.com

A video of Gilmore reading his poetry at The Rogue Theater in Tucson, Arizona is available on YouTube, which also includes readings of his poems by actors such as David Greenwood (who reads "Semper Fi" and "Prayer Wars"):

https://www.youtube.com/watch?v=Yfhb_0llrRU

Gilmore lives in Tucson, Arizona and divides his time between playing jazz, writing, and loving his children and grandchildren, his life partner JoAn, and his cat.

Artist's Bio

Gwen Murphy is an American artist and designer who, since childhood, has seen a presence in each pair of shoes—and thus in 2007, she began transforming worn-out and/or discarded shoes into wildly original and imaginative art, fantastic characters with faces and personalities of their own.

The image on this book's front cover, "Manifest Destiny," is from her Foot Fetish series of sculptures, and the pair of loafers belonged to her husband when he was a stockbroker. The title acknowledges the sad irony of a Native American moccasin style being appropriated for a shoe worn by a white-collar professional.

Murphy graduated with an MFA degree in Sculpture in 1990 from the Boston University College of Fine Arts. Her work has been widely exhibited in numerous cities in the United States and abroad, including Atlanta, Boston, Chicago, Hong Kong, Houston, Leipzig (Germany), Los Angeles, Miami, New York, Philadelphia, Pittsburgh, and Washington, DC.

The artist's blog includes numerous image galleries as well as details about her exhibitions:

http://www.gwenmurphy.com

For images and information about 15 of Murphy's Foot Fetish sculptures, please see "Old Shoes Reborn as Living Faces" by Simone Preuss in *Recycle Nation* (22 November 2010):

http://recyclenation.com/2010/11/shoes-reborn-recycling-living-faces

✧

Notes

www.ingramcontent.com/pod-product-compliance
Lightning Source LLC
Chambersburg PA
CBHW071314200626
46813CB00015B/2196